Earthquakes!

An Earthshaking Book on the Science of Plate Tectonics

Earth Science for Kids

Children's Earth Sciences Books

PRODIGYWIZARD
BOOKS

Buildings tremble, the ground shakes, the Earth cracks! An earthquake is a terrifying movement of the Earth's crust. Its powerful movement scares everyone and puts people into a panic.

Most of us think that the surface of the Earth is fixed and stable, so why does it shake?

The Earth's surface is constantly moving, but we don't notice most of its tiny movements. Our solid ground moves between one to six inches each year. For the land on Earth to move a significant distance, it takes millions of years.

Four layers make up the Earth. These are the inner core, outer core, mantle and crust. The mantle and crust are thin layers. Tectonic plates are the broken pieces of the thin skin. Imagine these plates as pieces of a puzzle. They float on top of the Earth's inner core.

Seven major plates cover most of the Earth. These plates may also include at least eight minor plates.

The seven major tectonic plates are the Antarctic, African, Eurasian, South American, North American, India-Australian and Pacific plates.

Some of the Earth's minor tectonic plates include the Scotia, Arabian, Caribbean and the Nazca plates.

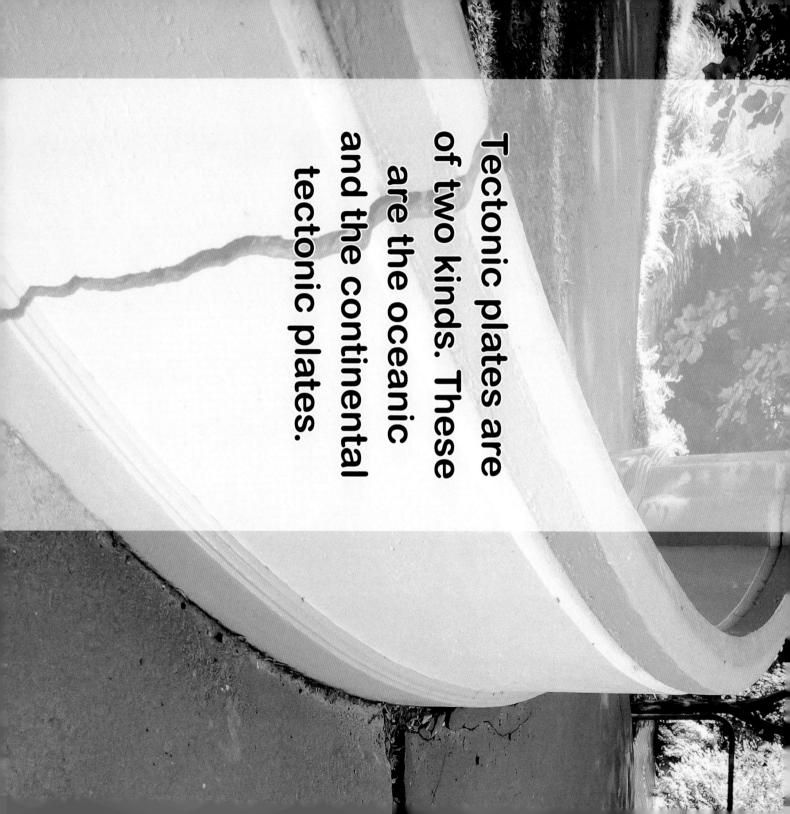

Tectonic plates are of two kinds. These are the oceanic and the continental tectonic plates.

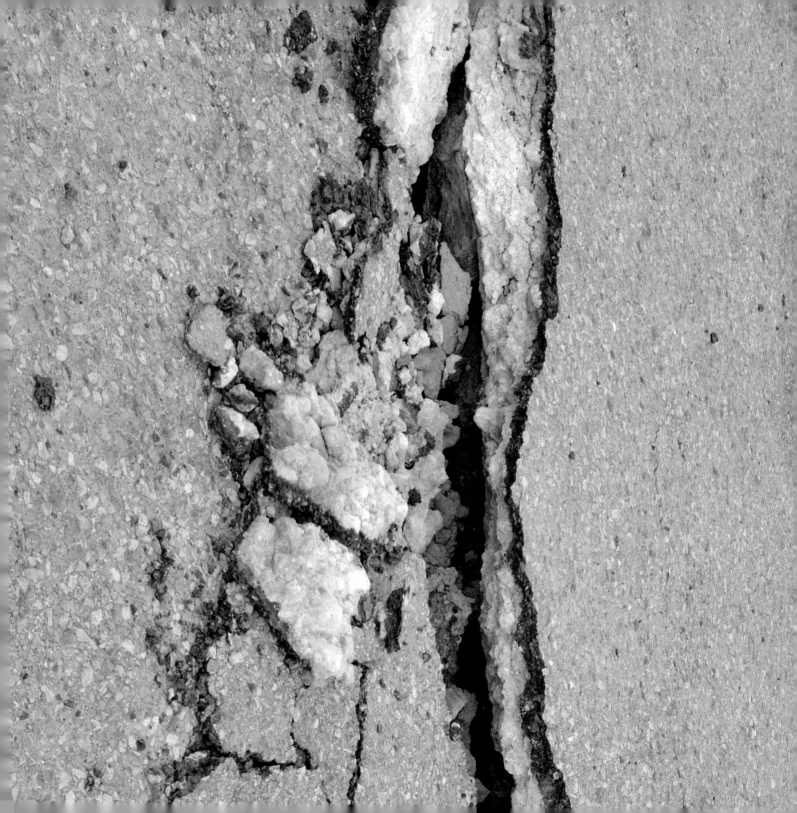

Oceanic tectonic plates are composed of oceanic crust, known as 'sima', which is made primarily of silicon and magnesium. That's why it is called "si-ma".

On the other hand, continental tectonic plates are composed of the continental crust known as "sial," which is primarily made up of silicon and aluminum.

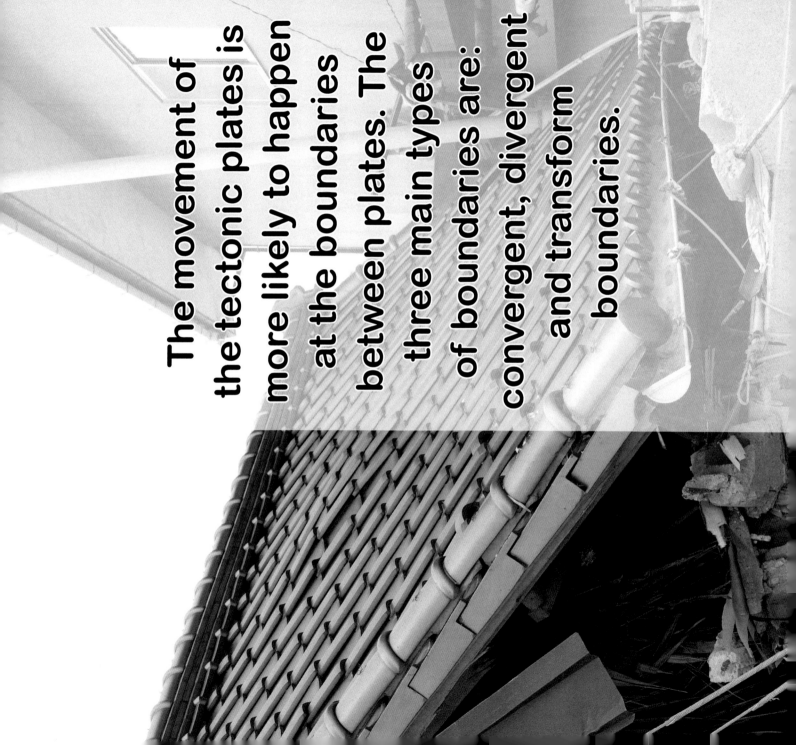

The movement of the tectonic plates is more likely to happen at the boundaries between plates. The three main types of boundaries are: convergent, divergent and transform boundaries.

Convergent Boundaries- In these boundaries, two tectonic plates push together. In this boundary, the two plates usually follow a subduction movement, where one plate will move under the other. The plates move slowly. Usually convergent boundaries are areas where mountain and volcanoes form, or areas with a lot of geological activities. These areas may have high earthquake activity.

Convergent Boundaries

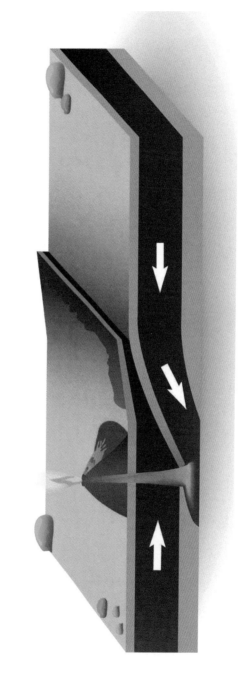

Divergent Boundaries

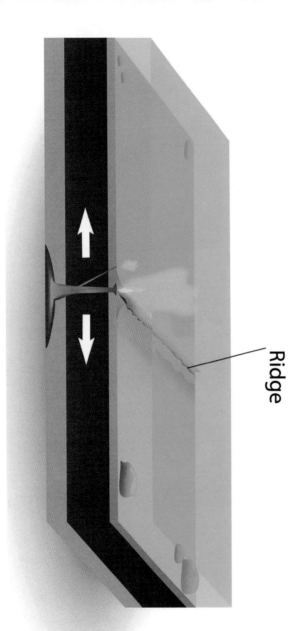

Ridge

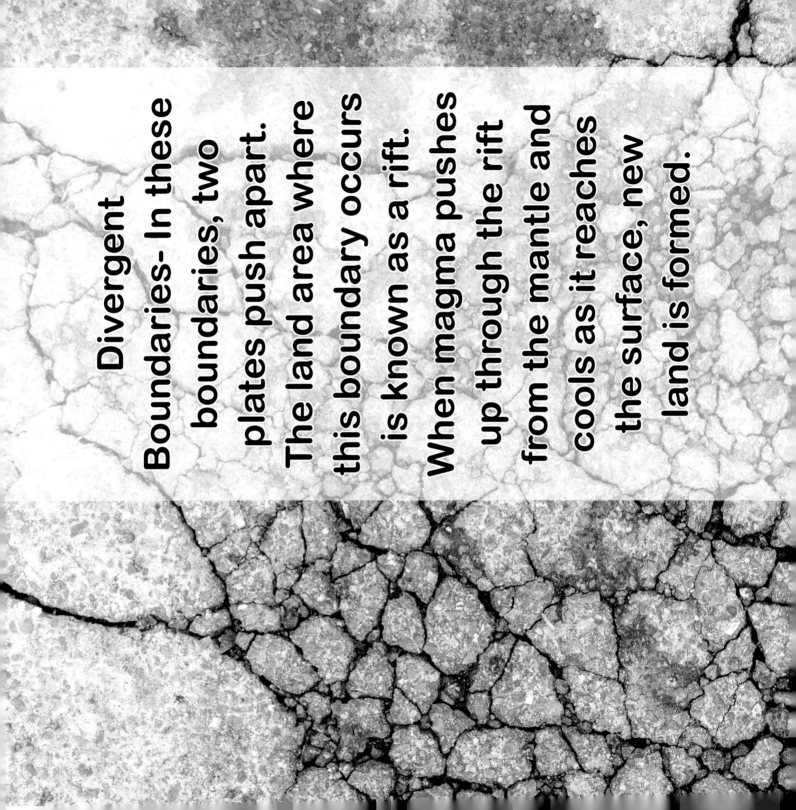

Divergent Boundaries- In these boundaries, two plates push apart. The land area where this boundary occurs is known as a rift. When magma pushes up through the rift from the mantle and cools as it reaches the surface, new land is formed.

Transform Boundaries- In these boundaries, the two plates slide past each other. The areas which have this kind of boundary are called faults. Earthquakes often occur in these areas.

Transform Boundaries

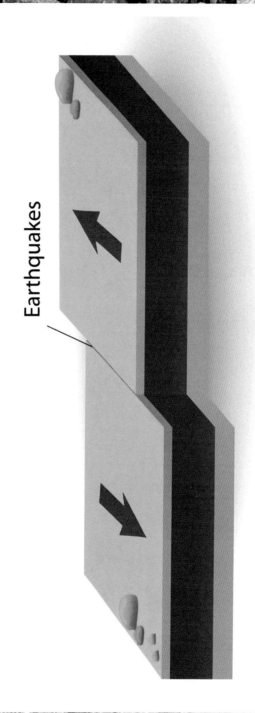

Earthquakes

The San Andreas Fault in California is one of the famous transform boundaries. It is between the North American Plate and the Pacific Plate. Many earthquakes in California are known to be caused by this fault.

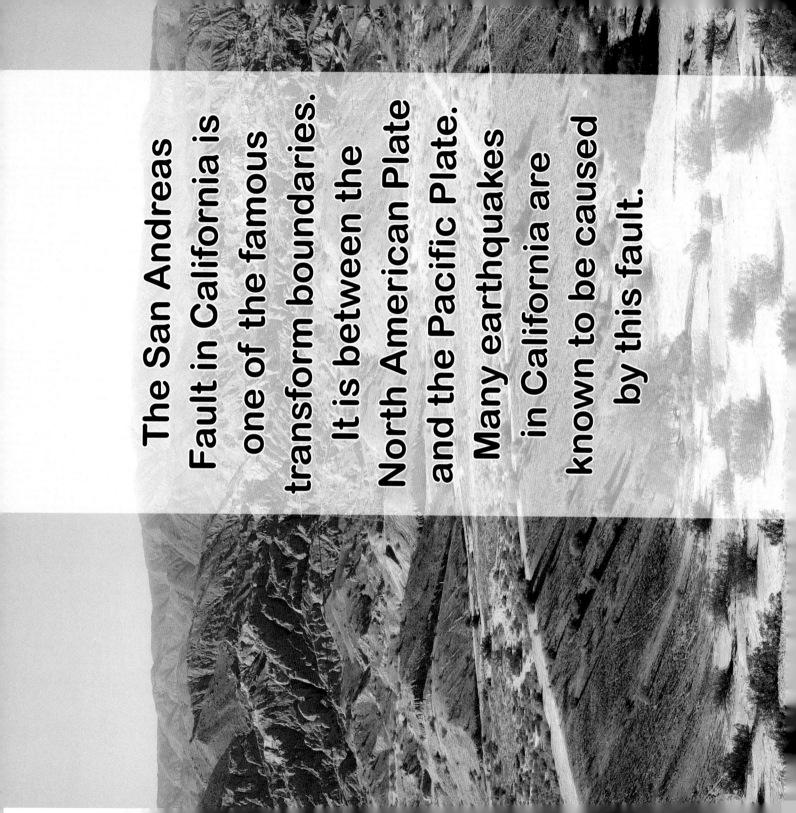

Do you know about the Mariana Trench? It is the deepest part of the ocean. The convergent boundary between the Pacific Plate and the Mariana Plate formed the Mariana Trench.

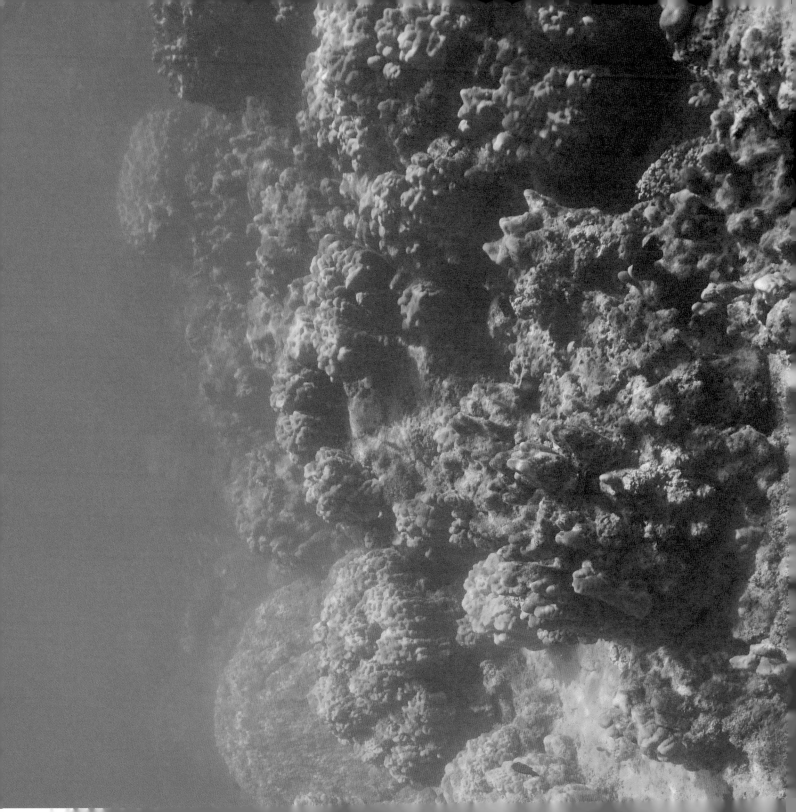

Do you know that the Convergent Boundary of the Indian Plate and the Eurasian plate make the Himalayan Mountains? It includes Mount Everest.

Seismologists are the scientists who study earthquakes. They can tell how serious an earthquake is by using a machine known as the seismogram. This machine rates the intensity of the earthquake.

Most people die in earthquakes because they are trapped in collapsed buildings. After an earthquake, tsunamis (huge waves of water), floods, fires and mudslides can happen. This can cause deaths of millions.

That is why it is very important to have fire and earthquake drills. This keeps us ready when earthquakes happen. We should know what to do if the ground starts to shake. Always remember to stay calm and not to panic. Presence of mind is highly recommended.

Made in the USA
Middletown, DE
24 July 2019